D1743474

ACROSS THE GULF
OF TIME

ACROSS THE GULF OF TIME

Evelyn Hooven

Published by New English Review Press
a subsidiary of World Encounter Institute
PO Box 158397
Nashville, Tennessee 37215
&
27 Old Gloucester Street
London, England, WC1N 3AX

Cover Art and Design by Kendra Mallock

ISBN: 978-1-943003-69-3

Library of Congress Control Number: 2022945726

First Edition

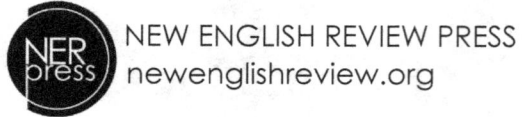

NEW ENGLISH REVIEW PRESS
newenglishreview.org

In loving memory of my father Nathan Golden,
a scholar reverent and true.

Contents

PART FIVE ". . . AS A DREAM OF STONE:"
TRANSLATIONS

FOUR AFTER NERVAL

FOUR AFTER BORGES

THREE WAYS OF SEEING THE MUSE

PART ONE

Images:

Love and Its Turnings

SONNET:
WINGLESS IN THE AIR

Wearied with moving without rest or wings
We seek some comfort from the solid ground,
Bereaved, we mourn the loss of sought-for things
Forever banned, now we are earthward bound.

Not comfort-craving moved us to descend
Nor poets' praise of earth nor want of pride,
Nor fear that heaven always would forfend
Man's entrance to the place where gods abide.

Only that we were wingless in the air
Defenseless, hurled about by angry wind,
Thrust out by the unfriendly atmosphere
To earth, by fiercer powers than we consigned.

May heaven grant to those who are still vain
The gifts it won't permit them to attain.

IN MEMORY OF

That night, we wove our way
With the white moon three fourths itself,
Seeing an ice-rink in the shape of a fish,
We looked among dank castles of cement
For an ocean at least.
Our shadows full of linden leaves were bare
Between trees except where we stepped
And wondered if they felt.
We stood where we could catch most light,
Closed our eyes to the ocean not there
And to ourselves outlined on concrete.
Summery clothed we are fleshed smooth white
And the sky is cool.
We can touch the trees,
Let the tide come after.
Look how our glance,
How it strikes the air.

Moons come round and castles fall
To the waves' dark taking.
All our chains rise strange and burning—
Dry the winding, white and fast.

MAGIC

Luck made us skeptical,
Our creatures—
Nonsense, terror, mystery—
Are gone from the mantel.
I look for you as for signals,
O Love, who is our enemy?
I look for you as for fields—
Everything's lost. . .

Is it
The distressed
Likenesses
Of monsters
Who will not
For abracadabra
Or sticks
Or stones
Ever quite die?

Is it the ancient dragon,
Hoarder of everything:
Wealth, strength, woe, time,
He who guards the bright cup
And likely sword,
He who threatens
The strange bird
That whirrs and calls
And disappears
Across coldest water?

ENIGMA 12/31

Former companion,
You are not
Who I thought. . .
Yet no use, none
In refusal
To admit
A difference still—
Your voice, how
It seems with you—
Those shadows
Approximations
Hold and follow—how
Are they made, nerves
I mean, what are they?

Are you ever
Sad or void
Absented from
Is it some shape
You once called
Love and struggle,
Or from knowledge
Of that shape
Instead of
A trailing off. . .

Traces
Frail, persistent
On an indistinct

Horizon—
Creatures
Nearly present
Nearly explosive—
What are they?

There are
Have been
Explanations
Too many
So none
Quite true
And happy
New year
To you, too.

MORNING SONG

Waking, crossing
This threshold
While you sleep there,
In plain November hunger
Gloom or candid glare
Something is missing.

Last week's singing
Holds no longer
Neither oblique gold
Nor garlands here
Oh I have wished all year
For what's astonishing.

FOR A COUPLE OCCASIONALLY ON THE VERGE OF SEPARATION:

A Poem in Six Movements

I

Sunlight through the picture doors.
Coffee, a spoon gleams
Against porcelain—
There is never enough time. . .
The household's baby stares
At grown strangers—
An expensive development, this—
Yards wide, trees half grown.
Cars live
Behind doors
Of burnt sienna, terra cotta,
Aquamarine.
Five minutes and lovely weather—
Faces strained from hours
Of trying to get through—
Genuine smiles—
Goodbye, enjoy the day.
The cars close and go.

Reading aloud
In Robert Frost
Brings the dark farmhouse.
A timelessness around us—
Are you happy?
Are you afraid?

Will you play with me?
Will you leave me alone?
There are such unmentionables—
There must be no taboos;
We shall talk freely
And not stir issues.
We should be closer
And further apart.
Open the door.
Shut the door?
Don't tell me your thoughts,
I want to relax.
Don't make threats
Or I'll go away.
I would like to go
But think I'll stay.

It is a theatre now.
Together, we are an audience.
We move gently, unfolding.
Holding thoughts lightly and with care
Like comrades who have worn one compass
Borne the identical scar.

(Time passes)

II
Past midnight at the airport.
Luggage is too late to care.
This is London,
Are you happy?
Let's sleep just anywhere—
Unburdened, defenseless. . .
Is something lost?

A book, a Spanish fan,
A contraceptive kit,
The baggage circles—
It will be the same. . .
The Whitman embrace
For humanity
United by objects,
Purpose, memory—
Celebration of patient assemblage—
Tender colors, variety. . .
Will it sustain us
Past dust and busses?
Past hands extended
Rarely in sympathy—
Will it clarify
The multiple address
Of subways or metros or tubes?

(Time passes)

    III
This candid morning—
Feathers cold or asunder—
No seagull stays.
Bread, glints of fish.
A promising rock—
Soaring—
Do not compel her. . .
The Lighthouse seems near—
Uncleansed glass,
Hornets, pillars shaken—
Not broken—
Can one find such locale
Desirable?

One can relish snapshots
Of worn and worn tides.

(Time passes)

IV

Below the tight bodice, a coral
Flow makes all shapes questionable.
What have I chosen?
The blank walls stare,
I cover them in bright paper
With my mind's eye.
Dream the eaves of birds,
Dream another age—
Four-posters uncurtained
Towards foliage
Vivid, serene. . .
What is loss?
What is blessing?
Does anyone know?
Is anyone home?

(Time passes)

V

I said yes because I was tired.
We made arrangements
According to rain, according to time;
Why open the nest of creatures
Angry, confined?
I feel the reins, the blackmail—
Face averted, fist on the wall,
Scarred by chains, dreaming—
Composure, figure in belted coat

Strap on the shoulder.
Hands do not reach for hands—
What is the matter?
Nothing's the matter.
Voices make no incursion.
We may not return
From this journey alive.
Wishes do not intervene—
Numbness extends its invasion. . .
Amnesia—
Petrification.

(Time passes)

    VI
We cannot remember
What caused us
To settle here—
We thought our charts
Docket
Insignia
Would carry us
Entirely elsewhere—
It strains our courage
To mention
A strange dream
Of pilgrimage
Past wheels
Past broken music boxes—
Past wheels
Past broken music boxes—
Let us attune the mind. . .
One must admit
That each terrain

Has its limit—
We need not admit
To discord in this land
Nor cease to remember
Nor cease to long for—
Rain, morsel, bloom. . .